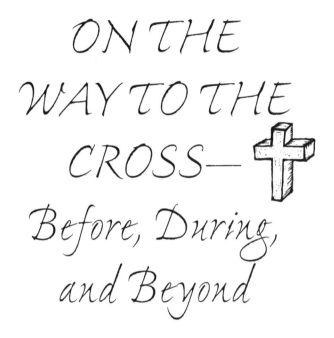

ON THE WAY TO THE CROSS—
Before, During, and Beyond

Dr. Patricia Louise Wilson

WESTBOW
PRESS®
A DIVISION OF THOMAS NELSON
& ZONDERVAN

Scripture taken from the King James Version of the Bible.

Scripture taken from the Holy Bible, NEW INTERNATIONAL VERSION®. Copyright © 1973, 1978, 1984, 2011 by Biblica, Inc. All rights reserved worldwide. Used by permission. NEW INTERNATIONAL VERSION® and NIV® are registered trademarks of Biblica, Inc. Use of either trademark for the offering of goods or services requires the prior written consent of Biblica US, Inc.

Scripture quotations taken from the Holy Bible, New Living Translation, Copyright © 1996, 2004. Used by permission of Tyndale House Publishers, Inc., Wheaton, Illinois 60189. All rights reserved.

All Scripture quotations in this publications are from The Message. Copyright © by Eugene H. Peterson 1993, 1994, 1995, 1996, 2000, 2001, 2002. Used by permission of NavPress Publishing Group.

Scripture quotations taken from the Holy Bible, New Living Translation, Copyright © 1996, 2004. Used by permission of Tyndale House Publishers, Inc., Wheaton, Illinois 60189. All rights reserved.

WestBow Press books may be ordered through booksellers or by contacting:

WestBow Press
A Division of Thomas Nelson & Zondervan
1663 Liberty Drive
Bloomington, IN 47403
www.westbowpress.com
1 (866) 928-1240

ISBN: 978-1-5127-2412-7 (sc)
ISBN: 978-1-5127-2413-4 (hc)
ISBN: 978-1-5127-2411-0 (e)

Library of Congress Control Number: 2015920664

Print information available on the last page.

WestBow Press rev. date: 01/06/2016

Dedication

This book is dedicated to my family
And all my Christian Friends
Who "walk the walk" with me

Forward

The Apostle Paul wrote, "I am crucified with Christ, nevertheless I live." In this powerful book by Patricia Wilson the reader is taken through the experience of the Passion Week, but not left there. She goes on to tell you how we can live when we have to experience life in such a way as to feel that the tomb is our only place to live. In this book we walk with Jesus so passionately described as the Messiah who came so that we could behold God in the flesh. We learn that He has already traveled down every road that we could find ourselves walking, and He leads us through the crises, the accidents, the unexpected troubles and tribulations. He shows us the way to eternal life as a life of eternal peace and an assurance of the Love of God. He was tested in all the ways that we have been tested. The author helps us to see His testing in light of our own, and by her own experiences. He was rejected, lied about, persecuted, and crucified; yet He lives. The great message of this book is that in dying to self we truly learn how to live and what is important in life. Our life is like a vapor, here today and gone tomorrow. Our eternal tomorrow is in Him, so when we have truly been crucified, dead, and buried; then we can rise in His resurrection life that can so permeate our being that we are living in the presence of His Throne Room, while still walking here on earth.

DOCTOR R. WAYNE MILLER, FOUNDER
CATHEDRAL BIBLE COLLEGE
MYRTLE BEACH, SOUTH CAROLINA

Contents

Chapter One

The Cross

◇◇◇◇◇

The crucifixion of Jesus, the Messiah, and the Son of God took place during the 1st century A.D. He was nailed to the cross. "What shall I do, then, with the one you call the king of the Jews? Pilate asked them. Crucify Him! They shouted. Why? What crime has He committed? Asked Pilate. But they shouted all the louder, Crucify Him!" (Mark 15:12-14 NIV). Jesus paid the ultimate price – He paid it all.

Just as Jesus had His own Cross to bear through His life on earth, we, too, must bear our own Cross (our spiritual Cross) throughout our earthly journey. In this regard I am not looking at the physical cross that was made of wood, but I am referring to the spiritual Cross. We need to take up our own Cross daily. We need to let go of and die to our sins. We die to our carnal part that is within our being of the way we think, the way we act, and the deeds that we commit that are not pure. We need to cleanse our souls with the blood of Jesus who died on the Cross for us because of our sins.

The Cross is very significant and is a symbol that has different distinct meanings for different people. I surveyed 10 people and asked the question, "What is the first thought that comes to your mind when I say, THE CROSS?" These are the responses I received.

1. Jesus
2. Salvation
3. Pain and suffering
4. Jesus died for me
5. Forgiveness
6. By His stripes we are healed
7. The greatest Love
8. Overcoming the grave
9. Going home to be with God
10. Fulfillment of prophesy

This is only a small sampling of what people think and feel about the Cross and the crucifixion. Needless to say, these responses are an accumulation of ideas that come from the crucifixion of Christ. My own thoughts and feeling about what the Cross represents is that Jesus, who represents God, is willing to die to atone for humanity's sin and make salvation possible. I have received so much more from thinking about the Cross. I think of Jesus when I am in a difficult situation. I think of Jesus when I am feeling humiliated. I think of Jesus when I am in deep emotional pain. I think of Jesus when I am needing to forgive someone. By my enduring all these things it seems very insignificant compared to what Jesus went through. Jesus went through so much more before the crucifixion, during the crucifixion, and then beyond the resurrection when He overcame the grave. There are people who do not believe in Jesus and are still crucifying His name.

The Cross has inspired many songs that are written to signify the meaning of the Cross. Hearing songs about the Cross actually soothes my soul, and reminds me of salvation and hope. Why? Because I know Jesus did it all for us sinners. Just by being human and living in the flesh says I/we are sinners.

The Cross does give me hope that I am redeemed by His blood.

The Cross gives me peace to know there is eternal life of my spirit and I am on the way to heaven after the death of my human body. The Cross shows me the ultimate in love that someone died for me to save my soul and to give me salvation.

Chapter Two
Before the Arrest

◇◇◇◇◇

What I am interested in is examining certain aspects during the days before the crucifixion and the time during the crucifixion, and then I want to compare what happened to Jesus and how it parallels what we go through during our life on earth. I want to show what life is like beyond the resurrection when Jesus overcame the grave.

I would like to start at the Lord's Supper where Jesus and His disciples gathered to eat the Passover. "On the first day of the Feast of Unleavened Bread, the disciples came to Jesus and asked, 'Where do you want us to make preparations for you to eat the Passover?" (Matt. 26:17 NIV) This is referred to as the Last Supper or the Lord's Supper. This is where Jesus informed his disciples that one of them will betray him. Keep in mind that Jesus had a purpose for everything He did and everything He said. Jesus knew that Judas would be His deceiver and betray Him before He was arrested.

Let's take the word "betray", and according to the Webster dictionary the meaning is: "to deliver to an enemy by treachery; to prove unfaithful." Vines Concise Dictionary of the Bible says, "to give over, to deliver to prison or judgment: and the noun 'traitors' as in Luke 6:16."

Even though Jesus knew what He must do because of all the sins in the world, it must have given him much sorrow to know one of his believers and followers would betray him and prove unfaithful.

This, too, is what we experience when we love and trust someone and find they are unfaithful. My experience was with my husband who had been unfaithful. The pain I experienced was unbearable and I knew it would destroy our marriage. There are other forms of betrayal that are in families, betrayal between friends, and between loved ones. I felt the agony and pain that pierced my heart. There was something I had to remember to get through all of this.

I knew that Jesus would forgive and look to His Father for the strength He needed to go on - - this is what I knew I needed to do, also. We need to follow Christ's example. A good question to ask, "What would Jesus do?" We, also, need to take it to the Lord in prayer. The Lord cares about you. "Cast all your anxiety on Him because He cares for you." (1 Peter 5:7)

Chapter Three

Before the Crucifixion

◇◇◇◇◇

I t is hard to imagine what it was like when Jesus was arrested and the torture He endured. "The men who were guarding Jesus began mocking and beating Him. They blindfolded Him and demanded, "Prophesy! Who hit you? And they said many other insulting things to Him" (Luke 22: 63-65 NIV). When He was beaten to the point of not being able to recognize Him, He not only endured physical pain, He was ridiculed. The Scripture according to Mark 15:19-20 NIV it says, "Again, and again they struck Him on the head with a staff and spit on Him. Falling on their knees, they paid homage to Him. And when they had mocked Him, they took off the purple robe and put His own clothes on Him. Then they led Him out to crucify him." During this time He had endured unending insult after injury and severe cruelty.

What our Savior went through was for the sinners of this world. He had the ability to withstand hardship because He obeyed His Father's plan and He knew that God's love for Him would get him through everything. Jesus Christ, the Son of God, paid the price – He paid it all for us.

Chapter Four

Take This Cup from Me

◇◇◆◇◇

Before the arrest of Jesus, according to Luke 22: 39-44, Jesus made an appeal for His case to His Father. When He went to pray on the Mount of Olives He appealed to His Father to take this all away from Him. "Jesus went out as usual to the Mount of Olives, and His disciples followed Him. On reaching the place, He said to them, 'Pray that you will not fall into temptation.' He withdrew about a stone's throw beyond them, knelt down and prayed, 'Father, if you are willing, take this cup from me; yet not my will, but yours be done.' An angel from heaven appeared to Him and strengthened Him. And being in anguish, He prayed more earnestly, and His sweat was like drops of blood falling to the ground." Jesus knew what His sentence was and yet He made his appeal to God to remove what was in store for Him, but Jesus knew it had to be God's will and not His own.

We as humans will pray to God when something goes wrong or there is a tragedy of some kind or even when someone leaves us. We have a tendency to beg and plead with God. Sometimes we will try to bargain with God and tell Him what we will do for Him if He will only change the situation or take away the bad situation that we find ourselves in. However, there are times when

God uses those situations to help us grow, and yes, even test us in order for Him to help us build character. Look what happened to Job when Satan took everything away from him and left him destitute. Job had all the faith in God and that faith kept him close to God and God stayed close to Job and never left him. In the end Job was favored by God and received a double portion of everything. God has a plan for all of us and we need to have faith in Him to see us through any situation. Jesus had faith in His Father and God had a plan for Jesus to save His children from sin when they believed that Jesus is the Son of God, and they have asked Him for His forgiveness because of their sins. We must believe that Jesus died because of our sins, ask forgiveness, believe that Jesus is the son of God, and then all who believe are born again.

Chapter Five

God's Plan and Purpose

◇◇◇◇◇

Jesus knew He had a purpose for being on earth – He knew because He is the Son of God. He knew what He had to endure during His time on earth before He went to be with God, His Father, and sit at God's right hand. "Yes, It is as you say," Jesus replied. "But I say to all of you: In the future you will see the Son of Man sitting at the right hand of the Mighty One and coming on the clouds of heaven" (Matt. 26:64 NIV). We, too, have a purpose and God has a plan for our lives.

"It's not about you. The purpose of your life is far greater than your own personal fulfillment, your peace of mind, or even your happiness. It's far greater than your family, your career, or even your wildest dreams and ambitions. If you want to know why you were placed on this planet, you must begin with God. You were born by his purpose and for his purpose.

The search for the purpose of life has puzzled people for thousands of years. That's because we typically begin at the wrong starting point – ourselves. We ask self-centered questions like, what do I want to be? What should I do with my life? What are my goals, my ambitions, my dreams for my future? But focusing on ourselves will never reveal our life's purpose. The Bible says, "It is God who directs the lives of his creatures; everyone's life is in his power"." (*The Purpose Driven Life* by Rick Warren, copyright date 2002 by Rick Warren. Use by permission of Zondervan, www.zondervan.com)

Jesus appealed to God "to take this cup from me." God had a plan and a reason for His ruling. In our court system there is an appellate court where people can appeal the decision from a lower court and ask that the case against them be removed or retried. This is a reprieve for those who are innocent. Man's court system is not without flaws and problems and is governed by the laws of man. However, God is the higher power and His law supersedes all laws of the land made by man. I have experienced court procedures in my lifetime and I know of the inadequacies that occur during a case before the court. It took two and a half years to settle one of my cases and I knew that God had it all in His hands. All I prayed for was for God to open the eyes of the judge and let him see the truth. In the end, God prevailed, the judge saw the truth, and I won my case. Of course I had to do my part and provide my attorney with all the necessary back up to substantiate my case. It was a hard and grueling effort to make sure that my i's were all dotted and all my t's were crossed. I had to do what it would take to put the truth in my attorney's hand who in turn would present it to the judge. Once I did my part then God could do the rest.

Chapter Six

God Carried Me

◇◇◇◇◇

T hinking back of how Jesus had to endure so very much after His arrest, my experiences seemed rather small in comparison. There was a time in my life that I endured physical pain at the hand of my father, my brother, and later from my husband, all of which I did not deserve this kind of treatment. During my childhood I was never given the "tools" by my parents to cope with what I was faced with in my lifetime. My parents did not go to church or read the bible to their children, but they did know there was a God. The one thing I can remember was my mother singing songs like: What a Friend We Have in Jesus, or Let Me Hide Myself in Thee, or The Old Rugged Cross. I remember a feeling of peace and love that grew inside of me whenever my mother sang those gospel songs.

I don't know how I knew at a very early age, that within my spirit there was a special knowing that there is a higher power to protect me. Of course that power is our Lord God Almighty. I did have an encounter with God at 3 years of age. I now know because I have had two more encounters with God to prove that He can supernaturally work in our lives the same way that He worked in Jesus's life during His time on earth.

I didn't realize the way that God works in our lives until I was much older. I was told by my mother, father, and grandmother that I was very close to death at that early age of 3. I was just hours away from death. It was late evening when the doctor arrived and after he examined me he told my parents and grandmother that I would be dead by morning. This was my first encounter with God.

It would be evident through several other similar events in my life that God was the power to supernaturally protect me, to heal me as well as guide me. The most significant supernatural healing I had in my life occurred in 2001 when I became deathly ill with meningitis and encephalitis. Either one can kill a person. And I had them both at the same time. I was in the hospital for 40 days and the doctors knew I was close to death. All the time I was in the hospital my husband never came to see me. My friend told me later that if I were a horse they would have shot me to put me out of my misery. The doctors could do nothing more for me, but God's supernatural power healed me. Even though my husband deserted me and was not there for me, I knew that I was not alone because God had never left me. I sing praises to Him every day and thank Him for all that He has done for me, and for what He continues to do for me. I do not want people to think that I am unique in this regard because it is true that God will do it for all His children.

What I am saying with all of this is that I have a miniscule awareness of what Christ went through when He suffered physically, mentally, emotionally, and spiritually throughout His life on earth. After all, it is very apparent that Jesus did not deserve this kind of treatment because even Pilate objected when the crowd yelled, "Nail him to a cross!" Pilate came back at the crowd and said, "Why? What crime has he committed?" (Mark 15:14 NIV). Was this Jesus's "day" in court? Did He get a fair trial? Did He get a chance to plead His case? In our court system some people are accused of crimes they did not commit, and then we find there are some who are sentenced to die or given a sentence of life in prison even though they are innocent. It must be a brutal consequence for those wrongly accused. That is a cross I never would want to bear. Jesus bore His Cross with all the dignity He could under the given circumstances. He kept His focus on God. Jesus knew the will of God and was willing to go all the way for whatever God directed Him to do. Keeping our focus on God can carry us through any circumstances, and no matter what life throws at us, we will overcome.

It was a subconscious and spiritual knowing on my part that there was more to life than I had been experiencing. In my early years, I did not know about the Christian walk. I was well in my thirties before I was baptized. It was obvious that I was acting out what I had learned from my parents in my years growing up. I was not attending church nor was I reading the bible. My marriage was similar to my parents' way of living. However, that encounter with God when I was a mere toddler did have a way with me to see life a little different from most children. Back then, I didn't know why I was not like most children, or why I saw things in a different light than other children. When I was in grammar school, I went to vacation bible school and learned about a man named Jesus. I immediately felt a "kinship" with Him. I learned that Jesus was here to show us how life as a true Christian should be lived. Even today I feel that I am different from most other people because of my bout with encephalitis and meningitis and being so very close to God in my near death experiences. In my wide circle of friends I find it hard to convey this supernatural healing that happened in my life. They just look at me with a blank stare as if I am from a different world. Only a few friends did say that I was a walking miracle.

I have often wondered how many other people grew up not knowing Jesus and how He saved us from our sins, or the miracles that He performed. So many people did not know how the Lord has been helping us in our everyday life, through our struggles, our crisis, our troubles, and turmoil. There is always something to remind us that God never leaves us. It may be a poem or it could be a song. It could be a spoken word that we hear. It could be the sound of a loved one's voice when they are talking to us.

We must be aware of all these things in order for us to realize it is God's way of letting us know He cares for us and will not leave us. Don't ever fear that God will walk away from you. His presence is constant and will strengthen you. His favor surrounds you like a shield so that evil cannot touch you.

While in my formative years I felt deserted by my parents - - not in the physical sense but in the emotional and spiritual sense. Parents sometimes don't realize how they can hurt a child deep in their soul. I know of this first hand when I was being abused by an older brother. My mother simply did not care and my father would leave to take long walks because he could not cope with some of the family problems. What it felt like at that time was my parents gave permission to the abuse that I endured because they did nothing to stop what was happening. This is what led me to believe they deserted me and I felt abandoned.

Carrying these feelings into adulthood, I knew I had to do something to correct this agony in my soul. My Lord, My God Jehovah is the total answer. He will never abandon His child. He will never leave at any moment, but He is there to carry me through thick and thin. I praise Him at all times during good times and during bad times. He is the one factor in my life that is constant and I can depend on Him being with me at all times.

So it is with any person who believes in Him, who obeys Him, and has taken Jesus as their personal savior.

Chapter Seven
The Right Choices

◇◇◇◇◇

For all of us humans on the way to the Cross, there are many struggles, turns, detours, and changes in direction, blockages, and other incidences that we have humanly created on our own. This will deter us from getting to our destination, and our destination is to be with our heavenly Father. Just as Jesus told us, "In my Father's house are many rooms; if it were not so, I would have told you. I am going there to prepare a place for you" (John 14:2NIV). Jesus is telling us that we will join Him someday in heaven.

Most of our struggles, changes, and harm are due to the choices that we make on a daily basis. If we can only realize that the choices we make today are going to affect our tomorrows. I consider having the freedom of choice as one of God's gifts He bestows upon us. Just like any of God's gifts, we are privileged to use them, but if we choose to abuse these gifts, we will have to pay the consequences. All through our lives there are consequences that we must pay for what it is we do. Each consequence does not have to be bad if we choose to live by God's law. If we choose to ignore His law and instead live a life that the world dictates, we will have consequences to pay. 1John 4:4-6 KJV says, "Ye are of

God, little children, and have overcome them: because greater is He that is in you, than he that is in the world. They are of the world: therefore speak they of the world, and the world heareth them. We are of God: he that knoweth God heareth us; he that is not of God heareth not us. Hereby know we the spirit of truth, and the spirit of error."

Jesus knew that there were choices He could make, but He always chose the Will of God in everything that He did. God gave Jesus the strength to endure what the people did that condemned Him and crucified Him on the Cross. Then they led Him off to Skull Hill. There was a man named Simon who came from the countryside, and was made to carry the Cross behind Jesus. The crowd followed and there were women weeping. Jesus told the women to cry for themselves and their children. Jesus was always concerned about others even in his deepest pain and weakness.

Chapter Eight
Up the Hill to Calvary

◇◇◇◇◇

"Traditionally the path that Jesus took with His Cross is called Via Dolorosa, meaning "Way of Grief" or "Way of Suffering." (Crucifixion of Jesus, Wikipedia, the free encyclopedia – "Path to the Crucifixion"). Jesus was losing blood, but He continued the three-hour walk through the city of Jerusalem to Golgotha on the way to Calvary to be crucified. How did Jesus get to the top of the hill where He was to be crucified? He could have called upon superhuman strength to continue up the hill to Calvary, however, He did not, but He knew that God was with Him every step of the way.

When we are involved with a certain situation; such as, rearing children and training them in the way they should go as it says in Proverbs 22:6 KJV, "Train up a child in the way he should go: and when he is old, he will not depart from it." We sometimes feel we are on an "uphill battle" to make sure they will be honest, loving, and responsible adults. No matter how difficult it is, or how tired and worn we are, this is one of our "hills to climb." Taking one day at a time and persevering through all the trials and tribulations we must remember that God is with us every step of the way. He will strengthen us as He did for Jesus in His walk up the hill to His destiny on Calvary.

Jesus did this because of the love He had for us – He was willing to die because of our sins. Would we as parents, who love our children so dearly, be ready to give our lives for them? Would we be able to make the ultimate sacrifice for them? Or even worse would we be willing to send our child to die for others? I dare not answer that question for other parents. I would have to do a lot of soul searching before I could answer that question for myself. In Genesis 22:2 NLT, God tested Abraham's faith – "Take your son, your only son – yes, Isaac, whom you love so much – and to the land of Moriah. Go and sacrifice him as a burnt offering on one of the mountains which I will show you." Abraham did as he was told, but before he killed his son, Isaac, God spared Isaac because Abraham proved to God that he was faithful and obedient to God's word.

Chapter Nine

The Day of the Crucifixion

◇◇◇◇◇

As recorded in the Gospels of Matthew, Mark, Luke, and John in the Holy Bible, it was the love for us that Christ Jesus died on the Cross to redeem us and save us from our sins. "Greater love hath no man than this, that a man lay down his life for his friends" (John 16:13 KJV).

When Jesus reached Calvary He was stripped of His garments and nailed to the cross. Here is Jesus, on what is referred to as "Skull Hill", to be crucified with two other men condemned to die on a Cross the same as Jesus. Jesus hung between the two common criminals. "Two other men, both criminals, were also led on with him to be executed. When they came to the place called the Skull, there they crucified Him, along with the criminals – one on his right and the other on His left" (Luke 23:32-33 NIV).

What transpired during that time was more humiliation, scorn, and mockery from religious leaders and the solders. Even the criminal on Jesus' left spoke ill of Jesus. "One of the criminals who hung there hurled insults at Him: "Aren't you the Christ? Save yourself and us!" But the other criminal rebuked him. "Don't you fear God," he said, "since you are under the same sentence? We are punished justly for we are getting what our deeds deserve. But this man has done nothing wrong." Then he said, Jesus, remember me when you come into your kingdom. Jesus answered him, "I tell you the truth, today you will be with me in paradise." (Luke 23:39-43 NIV).

Yes, when I think of Jesus I thought of how cruel people can be. There were times in my life when I thought of how I was treated. The one incident that comes to my mind is when my sister would tell my mother lies about me to take away any blame for something she had done. My mother would never ask me my side of the story, but she would condemn me for something I didn't do. Her words would cut right through me and I felt as if someone had struck me with a leather strap. She would always say to me after a severe scolding, "Patricia, you are the oldest and you should know better." It made me feel like I had to take on my sister's sin for whatever she did or whatever she would say.

Then one day when my sister and I were playing, my sister broke something. She yelled to our mother that Patricia broke something and it is not hers. Before our mother could respond, our father stepped in and told my sister he saw the whole thing and he told her that she lied. He told her that is wrong to accuse me of something I did not do. He told her in very stern words that he did not want her to ever lie like that again. When our father stood up for me and let my sister know she was at fault and lied to put the blame on me, I felt a great sense of relief that I did not have to carry the sins of my sister.

At that early age I didn't know I could give the situation over to the Lord. But if I had known Jesus and how He loved me and died for ALL sins of ALL people, I never would have carried another sin belonging to someone else. I would have known that Jesus paid the ultimate price and it is not my job to pay for another person's sin. It is my job to ask forgiveness for my sins, and forgive others as Jesus did as He hung dying on the Cross.

After Jesus was placed on the Cross between two criminals, He looked down from the cross. He looks upon the soldiers who tortured Him, scourged Him, mocked Him, and nailed Him to the

Cross. Is He not remembering His apostles and companions who have deserted Him? He probably remembers Peter who denied Him three times. Then there is the fickle crowd, who days before praised Him when in Jerusalem, and then days later chose Him to be crucified instead of Barabbas.

Can you imagine what was going through Jesus's mind? What were His thoughts as He watched the two criminals being nailed to their Crosses? How did it make Jesus feel when He heard the agonizing screams as the nails were driven into their bodies? What were some of the things Jesus could see as He waited His turn to be nailed to His cross? When Jesus lay down on the crossbeam and stretched out his arms, He knew He was the sacrificial lamb. He knew He was fulfilling His plan for which God sent Him to earth to do.

Chapter Ten

Forgiveness

◇◇◇◇◇

There are seven last things that Jesus expressed from the Cross before He breathed His last breath. At the height of His physical suffering His love prevails and right up to His last days on earth Jesus preaches forgiveness. He teaches forgiveness in the Lord's Prayer, "Forgive us our trespasses, as we forgive those who trespass against us." (Matt 6:12).

When Peter asks how many times we should forgive someone, Jesus answers, "Seventy times seven" (Matt 2:5). And from the Cross Jesus practiced what He preached. "Father forgive them for they do not know what they do" (Luke 23:24).

Forgiveness is a crucial thing. It is something I learned I *HAD* to do in order to earn my freedom from those who wronged me. At one time when I was praying, God spoke straight into my spirit and said, "There is no room in heaven for UNforgiveness." I knew I had a lot of work to do. That meant I would have to go back to my childhood and start a long list of everyone that had wronged me that I had not conscientiously forgiven.

One important thing I learned is that to just "think" with my mind that I forgave someone was NOT true forgiveness. It had to go deeper. Anyone can "say" I forgive you, but if it does not come from the heart, it is NOT a sincere forgiveness. When this became a reality to me, I then started to say, "Lord, I forgive Merrill (or any other person's name) from the bottom of my heart." Once I started forgiving from the deeper part of my being, I received a freedom I never felt before. It then occurred to me that whenever I forgave someone, it was for myself and not for the person that I was forgiving. I no longer was carrying that burden that was not mine and I obtained my freedom and gained peace of mind.

The wonder of Jesus's forgiveness is that when He forgives us, all of our past sins are forgiven. He no longer remembers our past sins and gives us a new clean slate to write our life on. This does not mean we can go out and keep sinning and expect Jesus to forgive us every time. There will be consequences to pay for choosing the life of sin; however, when we are forgiven, believe we are forgiven and live our lives in the way so we do not keep committing more sin. We will have a new beginning to walk the path with Jesus On the Way to the Cross.

Chapter Eleven

Paradise

◇◇◇◇◇

The second thing Jesus expressed from the Cross before He died was directed to the criminal on His right side. "Truly, I say to you, today you will be with me in Paradise" (Luke 23:43). The criminal on His right side is the one who speaks up for Jesus when he said, "This man has done nothing wrong." Then the criminal who was to His right who was a sinner repented with all his faith in Jesus. He turned to Jesus and asked - - "Jesus, remember me when you come in your kingdom" (Luke 23:42). In spite of the suffering that Jesus endured He responded as written in the Gospel of Luke, "Truly, I say to you, today you will be with me in Paradise."

We too will be in paradise with Jesus when we have taken Jesus as our personal savior, believe that He is the Son of God, believe that He died for us because of our sins, and ask Him to forgive us. It is then that we will be able to come into Paradise and the kingdom of heaven.

Chapter Twelve

A Mother's Heart

◇◇◇◇◇

Then the third expression that Jesus said from the cross, "Jesus said to His mother: 'Woman, this is your son.' Then He said to the disciple: 'This is your mother'." (John 19:26-27). Mary, the mother of Jesus, was with Him at the beginning of His ministry and now at the end of His public ministry at the foot of the Cross. Her mother's heart felt so much sorrow to see her son mocked, tortured, and crucified. It must have felt like a sword piercing Mary's soul to be an eye-witness to all of this.

This reminds me of a friend of mine. Bonnie had a son who had a heart problem in his adult life. Bonnie, his mother, being distressed over her son's health, prayed for him daily. Her son had six minor heart attacks. Bonnie told me she made it through her sorrow when she remembered Jesus on the Cross dying and Mary, His mother, watching her son die a cruel and gruesome death. Bonnie gave her son to God when he suffered his seventh and final heart attack. She was devastated, of course, but she derived comfort from Mary, the mother of Jesus. Mary watched her son suffer unbearably, but Bonnie's son left quickly and peacefully. Bonnie was grateful for that.

There were four there at the foot of the cross, Mary, His

mother, John, the disciple whom He loved, Mary of Cleopas, His mother's sister, and Mary Magdalene. In fact, He is addressing His third saying to Mary and John. Jesus is more concerned about taking care of His mother. Again, He rises above the occasion and thinks of those who are there who love Him. He wants to make sure His mother is taken care of, and John is the chosen one to look after Mary. The disciple, John, accepted her as his own mother.

Chapter Thirteen

My God, My God!

◇◇◇◇◇

The fourth expression from Jesus on the cross is, "My God, My God why have you forsaken me" (Matt 27:46 and Mark 15:34)? Both Gospels of Matthew and Mark related it was the ninth hour, after 3 hours of darkness that Jesus cried out this fourth saying from the Cross.

This cry from Jesus reflects the painful heart of the "human" Jesus. He must feel deserted by His Father and the Holy Spirit. I am sure He felt deserted by His earthly companions and the Apostles as well. He is now all alone, and He must face death by himself. This reminds me of a saying that goes something like this: You have to walk that lonesome valley, you have to walk it by yourself – No one else can walk it for you, you must go there by yourself. We too are all alone at the time of our death! Jesus completely lives the human experience as we do, and by doing so, He frees us from the clutches of sin when He gave His life on the Cross.

I had a friend, Tom, who had polio. He looked to me as his true friend. He lived alone and he had very few friends left that he had before the time he had polio. His sentiment about his friends was, "When the chips are down you can count your friends on one hand and have fingers left over." How true this is not only in my own experiences, but when I look to Jesus - - there He was hanging on the Cross and He could count His friends on one hand and have "fingers left over."

By the time that Jesus was so full of the sins from all mankind, it made me wonder if God was so much against sin, that He did forsake the "human" Jesus. The burden of all the sins of humanity for a moment overwhelmed the humanity of our Savior. The sins of the world were being felt by Jesus and I can truly see how He would cry out in the belief that He was forsaken.

This I am sure of is that there are countless people who actually feel that God has forsaken them. My sister is one of them. I felt pain when she would condemn God because He didn't take away her allergies. At one time she told me she hated God. I couldn't believe my ears because I never expected to hear those words come out of my sister's mouth. I felt pain throughout my body when I heard those words. God was not the blame for her allergies. Satan worked on her so badly she suffered from a whole list of allergies. She could not receive the Lord's magnificent healing power when she was blaming Him for her illness. Consequently she felt that God had forsaken her, but in reality it was the other way around. She had forsaken Him. She always wanted to blame God (or even someone else) for whatever the situation in which she found herself.

It was a dreadful moment in history when Jesus, who came to save us, is crucified. But does this really not have to happen? It is the Divine plan of His Father to defeat Jesus' humanity for God's plan to be completed and then to resurrect Him from death. We are redeemed by His death. "For there is one God. There is also one mediator between God and the human race, Christ Jesus, Himself human, who gave Himself as ransom for all"(1 Timothy 2:5-6). When Jesus died on the Cross we have been redeemed. If it were not for the Cross we would all go to be in hell.

Chapter Fourteen

"I Thirst," "It is Finished"

◇◇◇◇◇◇

When Jesus spoke His Fifth expression, "I thirst" (John 19:28), from the Cross it is a saying that shows His physical suffering is at a peak and He must be in shock. The wounds inflected upon Him in the scourging, the crowning of thorns, and the nailing upon the cross are taking their toll. He lost blood on the three-hour walk through the city of Jerusalem to Golgotha on the way to the hill where He would be nailed to the Cross and be crucified. "He himself bore our sins in his body upon the cross, so that, free from sin, we might live for righteousness. By his wounds you have been healed" (1 Peter 2:24).

"A jar of wine vinegar was there so they soaked a sponge in it, put the sponge on a stalk of hyssop plant, and lifted it to Jesus' lips. When He had received the drink, Jesus said, "It is finished." With that He bowed His head and gave up His spirit" (John 19 29-30). The sixth expression is Jesus' recognition that his suffering is over and His task is completed. Jesus is obedient to the Father and gives His love for mankind by redeeming us with His death on the Cross.

Chapter Fifteen

The Passover Lamb

◇◇◇◇◇◇

I n our society today we hear through the news media about cruel and abusive act people inflict on others. I even think of prisoners of war and how cruel interrogation techniques from the enemy are used upon prisoners. Hate crimes are committed all over the world, but the Brutal acts inflicted on our Savior to the bitter end was for everyone's salvation. He loved us as no one else could ever love us. Jesus paid the full price - - He paid it all!

"Jesus cried out in a loud voice, Father, into your hand I commend my spirit." (Luke 23:44) This is the seventh expression and the final saying of Jesus on the Cross. He died at the ninth hour (three o'clock in the afternoon), approximately at the time as the Passover lambs were slaughtered in the temple. Christ became the Passover Lamb as noted in 1 Corinthians 5:7, "For Christ our Passover Lamb has been sacrificed." It was because of our sins that the innocent Lamb was slain. Jesus fulfilled His mission and purpose for which His Father had sent Him to earth to do.

What the Cross represents is a powerful message to all of us. Yet, there are people who doubt the message of the Cross. There are people who do not believe that Jesus is the Son of God. There are people who do not believe that Jesus died because of our sins. There are people who do not believe that Jesus rose again from the dead. There are people who do not know that they are forgiven of their sins when all they need to do is ask. And there are people who believe that the Cross is nothing but dead wood from a tree.

If the unbelievers could only realize that Jesus Christ is the Son of God, and believe He died for us because of our sins, ask forgiveness, and believe He rose again, it would be their first step in their journey On the Way to their Cross that leads them to paradise and the kingdom of God.

Chapter Sixteen
God So Loved the World

◇◇◇◇◇

The meaning of the Cross is so much deeper and has spiritual connotation. The love that it portrays when you look beyond the physical pain and suffering and know that was the reason Jesus paid the full price. "For God so loved the world that He gave His one and only Son, that whoever believes in Him shall not perish but have eternal life" (John 3:16 NIV). In the NIV Message Bible it says, "This is how much God loved the world. He gave his Son. And this is why: so that no one need be destroyed by believing in Him, anyone can have a whole and lasting life. God didn't go to all the trouble of sending His Son merely to point an accusing finger, telling the world how bad it was. He came to help, to put the world right again. Anyone who trusts in Him is acquitted; anyone who refuses to trust Him has long since been under the death sentence without knowing it. And why? Because of that person's failure to believe in the one-of-a-kind Son of God when introduced to Him" (John 3:16-18 NIV Message Bible).

Some people don't even know that the love of God for them is unconditional and it is all encompassing. The beauty part of God's love for them is that no one has to do anything to earn that love. God created us with His love. He created us to have a relationship with Him. God longs for a relationship with us. In the book, "The Relationship Principles of Jesus", by Tom Holladay, Rick Warren who wrote the Book, "The Purpose Driven Life", wrote the forward to Tom Holladay's book.

Rick says, *"Learning to love God and others is to be our highest goal, our greatest aim, our first priority, our deepest aspiration, our strongest ambition, our constant focus, our passionate intention, and the dominant life value of our lives. The more we learn how to 'love authentically', the more like Jesus we become."* (*The Relationship Principles of Jesus by Tom Holladay, copyright date 2008 by Tom Holladay. Use by permission of Zondervan. www. zondervan.com*)

Looking at Jesus and what His greatest commandment is, Jesus answered the question by saying, "The most important one is this; Hear, O Israel, the Lord our God, the Lord is one. Love the Lord your God with all your heart and with all your soul and with all your mind and with all your strength. The second is this: Love your neighbor as yourself. There is no commandment greater than these" (Mark 12:29-31 NIV).

To "love authentically" is something we need to strive to do in our lives. There are many people that could not explain love let alone give love that is unconditional. Maybe this is due to how we experienced love in our formative years. If children are not provided the right environment to grow in love, then as adults they cannot give nor receive love in a manner that is free-flowing and unconditional.

As a child I longed to hear my parents tell me that they loved me. They thought that it was enough to provide a roof over my head, put food in my belly, and provide clothes for my back. It was enough for them to "show" their love for me and the other children in the family. They neglected to tell their children that they loved them, and to express that love so that their children could understand their love.

As an adult, my hunger to be told by my parents that they

loved me had grown to a point I had to do something to ease this longing. I started to read about love to help myself understand what I was missing. I started reading books on love and I found myself taking notes and filling a notebook full of loving and living notes from some of the books. All it did was wet my appetite to know more about love. Even though the books gave me insight into loving and they gave me explanations of why or why not a person choses to give love or to receive love, it still was not enough for me.

My search continued and I was constantly looking on the outside of myself for the love I was longing for. So I started to pray about love and to meditate on love. It was through my own effort that it all started to reveal the thing for which I spent so much time searching on the outside of myself. During one of my meditations (meditation to me is "listening" to God), I was focusing on God and His love. Then it was God who spoke into my spirit and told me what I was to do to find love. It was clear and precise that these words came to me, "Become What You Are Seeking!"

I kept repeating what God spoke to me, and I kept saying over and over again, "Become What You Are Seeking", in order to get it down in my soul. I started questioning what did this mean, and how can I use it? Then the light in my mind started flickering and finally the light directed me to God's Word. The book I needed was the Bible. The Bible that I owned had a concordance in the back of the book. To my amazement there was scripture after scripture with the words, "love", "loved", "loves," etc. I wondered where to start. I stuck my finger on the page and that is how I chose the first scripture to read, 1 Cor. 13. I read and reread it many times. I feel this is worth repeating the whole chapter in full.

1 Corinthians 13:1-13 KJV

"Though I speak with the tongues of men and of angels, and have not charity, I am become as sound

brass, or a tinkling cymbal. And though I have the gift of prophecy, and understand all mysteries, and all knowledge; and though I have all faith, so that I could remove mountains, and have not charity, I am nothing. And though I bestow all my goods to feed the poor, and though I give my body to be burned, and have not charity, it profiteth me nothing. Charity suffereth long and is kind; charity envieth not; charity vaunteth not itself, is not puffed up, seemly, seeketh not her own, it not easily provoked, thinketh no evil. Rejoiceth not in iniquity, but rejoiceth in the truth; beareth all things, believeth all things, hopeth all things, endureth all things. Charity never faileth: but whether there be prophecies, they shall fail; whether there be tongues, they shall cease; whether there be knowledge, it shall vanish away. For we know in part, and we prophesy in part. But when that which is perfect is come, then that which is in part shall be done away. When I was a child, I spake as a child, I understood as a child, I thought as a child; but when I became a man, I put away childish things. For now we see through a glass, darkly; but then face to face; now I know in part, but then shall I know even as also I am known. And now abideth faith, hope, charity, these three; but the greatest of these is charity."

When I looked in the NIV, the NLT, and NIV Message Bible, "Love" was used in place of the word "charity." Now I know what God was telling me. I needed to become love in order to experience love the way He intended it to be for all mankind. I read and reread 1 Cor. 13 many times because I wanted it to become a part of me. I wanted to live the way God's Word tells us to live. After this major revelation about love, I started wondering what else could God mean by, "Become What You Are Seeking!"

I found this to be an unending process to find all that I was seeking. My research started with The Cross. Then I turned to Jesus Himself. He is the truth, the way and the life. He is the perfect example of becoming the Word of God!

Chapter Seventeen

Become What You Are Seeking

◇◇◇◇◇

This time I looked at the Cross. There was more than one way to look at the meaning of the Cross. It seemed that most people focused on the humiliation, the scorn, the betrayal, the rejection, the desertion, the pain of being beaten unmercifully; but I know there is another side of the story. Just like there are two sides of a coin, there is another side of the Cross. There is power in the Cross. I wanted to know what Jesus would say to us to enable us to know the wonder of Him being raised from the dead. If there is more for me to know in order for me to become what I was seeking, I knew that Jesus would have the message for me. I believe that He must have ALL the answers to ALL that we are seeking. I looked at the time before His crucifixion. Jesus was talking to His disciples to explain to them that their Grief will turn to Joy! In John 16:19-22 NIV, "Jesus saw that they wanted to ask him about this so he said to them, 'Are you asking one another what I meant when I said, 'In a little while you will see me no more, and then after a little while you will see me'? I tell you the truth; you will weep and mourn while the world rejoices. You will grieve, but your grief will turn to joy. A woman giving birth to a child has pain because her time has come;

but when her baby is born she forgets the anguish because of her joy that a child is born into the world. So with you: Now is your time of grief, but I will see you again and you will rejoice, and no one will take away your joy."

This scripture went deep within my being and it set up a new way for me to believe and think about God's gifts. No one can take away anything from me that is from God. The Love I longed for – the Joy of living, and the peace that passes all understanding became a part of me. "Rejoice in the Lord always. I will say it again: Rejoice! Let your gentleness be evident to all. The Lord is near. Do not be anxious about anything, but in everything, by prayer and petition, with thanksgiving, present your requests to God. And the peace of God, which transcends all understanding, will guard your hearts and your minds in Christ Jesus" (Phil 4: 4-7 NIV). Then I realized that they are all mine and no one can take away that which God has given to me. In Gal 5:16, it tells us "So I say, live by the Spirit, and you will not gratify the desires of the sinful nature." And again in Gal 5:22-23, "But the fruit of the Spirit is love, joy, peace, patience, kindness, goodness, faithfulness, gentleness and self-control. Against such things there is no law." Now I could stop my searching on the outside of myself because it is all now on the inside of my soul. Thanks to Jesus I became what I was seeking!!!

Chapter Eighteen
After Three Days

◇◇◇◇◇

Let us now take a look at what happens beyond the Cross, and that is the resurrection. This is God's plan all along to defeat Satan's sinful hold on God's people. Most people get stuck on the crucifixion of Jesus and not the resurrection. After Jesus said "Father into your hands I commit my spirit." It was after saying this that He breathed His last breath. "At that moment, the temple curtain was ripped in two, top to bottom. There was an earthquake, and rocks were split in pieces." (Matt 27:51 NIV message bible) "When the centurion and those with him who were guarding Jesus saw the earthquake, and all that had happened, they were terrified and exclaimed, 'Surely He was the Son of God.'" (Matt 27:54) Yes, indeed, God's plan is in full motion. God's Glory is coming with the resurrection.

A wealthy man came to Pilate and asked for the body of Christ. His name was Joseph who became a disciple of Jesus. Joseph took the body and wrapped it in clean linens and placed the body of Christ in his own tomb. Then they rolled a large stone across the entrance of the tomb.

The chief priest and the Pharisees remembered when Jesus was alive that He told them, "After three days I will rise again."

The priests and Pharisees went to Pilate and asked him to order the tomb sealed - - They thought there was a good chance His disciples will come and steal the corpse and claim He was risen from the dead. Pilate said there would be a guard at the entrance to the tomb, and to go ahead and seal it the best you can.

When I think about the way most Christians handle the death of a family or friend, it is in most cases, they have a funeral home to make the arrangements. Then there is the showing where friends and family can come to greet the family of the departed to express their condolences. Then there is the funeral ceremony and the procession to the grave site where the departed is entombed or the coffin is lowered in the ground with a final good bye. This gives time for the healing process to start to take place for family and friends.

When I look at how the burial of Jesus took place and at the tomb where Jesus was laid to rest, Mary Magdalene and the other Mary were the ones sitting opposite the tomb. They later went to worship on the Sabbath. "After the Sabbath, at dawn on the first day of the week, Mary Magdalene and the other Mary went to look at the tomb. There was a violent earthquake, for an angel of the Lord came down from heaven and going to the tomb, rolled back the stone and sat on it. His appearance was like lightening, and his clothes were white as snow. The guards were so afraid of him that they shook and became like dead men. The angel said to the women, 'Do not be afraid, for I know that you are looking for Jesus, who was crucified. He is not here; He has risen just has He said. Come and see the place where He lay. Then go quickly and tell his disciples; He has risen from the dead and is going ahead of you into Galilee." (Matt 28:1-7) So the eleven disciples met with Jesus in Galilee. Then Jesus told them, "God authorized and commanded me to commission you: Go out and train everyone you meet far and near in this way of life, marking them by baptism in the threefold name: Father, Son, and Holy Spirit. Then instruct them in the practice of all I have commanded you. I'll be with you as you do this, day after day after day, right up to the end of the age." (Matt 28:18-20)

Chapter Nineteen

Receiving the Holy Spirit

◇◇◇◇◇

Jesus, the greatest teacher of all, has so much more to teach us. Jesus told His disciples that there would be someone else to teach them, to guide them, to strengthen them, and to love them. It was at the time when Jesus had risen and appears to His disciples. "Jesus came and stood among them and said, 'Peace be with you!' After He said this, He showed them his hands and side. The disciples were over joyed when they saw the Lord. Again Jesus said, 'Peace be with you! As the Father has sent me, I am sending you.' And with that He breathed on them and said 'Receive the Holy Spirit. If you forgive anyone his sins, they are forgiven; if you do not forgive them, they are not forgiven'" (John 20:19-20 NIV). Even before the crucifixion of Jesus when He was still teaching His disciples He said, "All this I have spoken while still with you. But the Counselor, the Holy Spirit, whom the Father will send in my name, will teach you all things and will remind you of everything I have said to you" (John 14:25-26 NIV).

We, too, have access to the Holy Spirit. For those who are believers and have been saved by our Savior will know of the Holy Spirit. The Scriptures are clear about our state and our sinful nature, but there is hope we have of eternal life through

Jesus Christ who came and died for us. The Holy Spirit inspired all Scripture. In 2 Peter 1:20-21, "Knowing this first, which no prophecy of the scripture is of any private interpretation. For the prophecy came not in old time by the will of man; but holy men of God spake as they were moved by the Holy Ghost." Even during the Old Testament and thousands of years before Jesus would be born, the Holy Spirit was speaking through the prophets about Christ's coming. "My dwelling place will be with them. I will be their God, and they will be my people" (Ezekiel 37:27).

Before John the Baptist was to baptize Jesus in the river, John spoke of Jesus and the Holy Spirit. In Mark 1:7-8 NIV, John the Baptist was talking to the people of Jerusalem, And this was his message: "After me will come one more powerful than I, the thongs of whose sandals I am not worthy to stoop down and untie. I baptize you with water, but He will baptize you with the Holy Spirit."

I have had an encounter with the Holy Spirit when I needed help. At one time in my life I started smoking, and after a couple of years I wanted to stop. I found that I couldn't do this on my own. I cut back on the amount of smoking that I was doing. I chewed gum thinking I could replace one habit with another. I would make myself wait before I would light another cigarette. I would not smoke in the house so I would always go outside – even when it was freezing outside of the house. I tried changing brands thinking that it would taste different and then I would not want to smoke.

One day when I was driving home and then pulled into the garage, I looked at the cigarette pack on the passenger seat beside me. I asked that cigarette pack, "How am I going to quit smoking you forever?" I sat there a minute when suddenly I just started talking to the Holy Spirit. "Holy Spirit please come to me. Enter into my entire body. Enter in every cell, fiber, and tissue of my body and cleanse everything that should not be there. Take it away. Take away everything that does not belong to me." I prayed for a little longer and then I just sat there. I didn't know what to expect so I sat there not thinking about anything. I then decided to get out of the car. I opened the door, and put one foot on the garage floor. I felt a magical sensation starting at the top of my head and cascading downward with a tingling sensation. I froze in that position and the sensation continued all the way down until it left from my feet. The first words from my mouth were, "Thank you!" From that moment on I never desired nor did I ever want another cigarette. It was my proof that the Holy Spirit can work in my life and will be there for anyone who believes and asks. In John 15:7 it says, "If you remain in me and my words remain in you, ask whatever you wish, and it will be given you." Then again in Matt 7:7-8, "Ask and it will be given to you; seek and you will find; knock and the door will be opened to you. For everyone who asks receives; he who seeks finds; and to him who knocks, the door will be opened."

Chapter Twenty

Getting to Know the Holy Spirit

◇◇◇◇◇

The often neglected person in teaching, and is actually the most important is the Holy Spirit. Who is the Holy Spirit? He is a person just as the Father and the Son. The Holy Spirit is part of the Holy Trinity. We know God is three in one. Three very distinct Persons make up the Godhead. They are all equal in every way. Even though it is not written in the bible, the "Holy Trinity" has become the reference of the three that make up the Godhead.

The Holy Spirit who inspired the Word of God through the prophets is also vitally interested in teaching the Word that we may obey it - - that results is spirituality, it produces growth, it produces maturity, and also produces effective ministry. All these things are what we need to strive for, and the Holy Spirit is always available to see us through in our endeavors to continue to grow, to become mature, and be effective in spreading the word and showing others the way to salvation.

The Holy Spirit was on the scene long before the day of Pentecost. He moved upon the face of the waters and was the active agent in creation. As it explains in Genesis 1:2, "And the earth was without form, and void; and darkness was upon the face of the deep. And the Spirit of God moved upon the face of the waters." The Holy Spirit was active and moved from the very beginning of time, whereas Jesus is the WORD and the Spirit MOVED. The Holy Spirit gave us the Word of God. As in 2 Peter 1:20-21 it says, "Knowing this first that no prophecy of the scripture is of any private interpretation. For the prophecy came not in old time by the will of man; but holy men of God spake as they were moved by the Holy Ghost." In the administrative council of the Trinity (The Father, Son and Holy Spirit) the Holy Spirit has been assigned by the Father and the Son the responsibility of application of THE TRUTH OF GOD!

There was some confusion over the identity of the Holy Spirit. Some of this dates back to the King James translation of the bible where the word "Spirit" or "Ghost" was used instead of "Breath" or "Wind" of God. Some even thought of the Holy Spirit as a "thing" rather than a Person. It seems that the life, death, and resurrection of Jesus Christ became more of the focal point in the Christian ministry which has been emphasized more than the workings of the Holy Spirit. In fact, the Holy Spirit has always worked hand in hand with Jesus Christ.

First is the Birth of Jesus – Matt. 1:20, "But while he thought on these things, behold the angel of the Lord appeared unto him in a dream, saying, Joseph, thou son of David, fear not to take unto thee Mary thy wife; for that which is conceived in her is of the Holy Ghost." Second the life and ministry of Jesus – Luke 4:1, "And Jesus being full of the Holy Ghost returned from Jordan, and was led by the Spirit into the wilderness..." AND ...Luke 4:18, "The Spirit of the Lord is upon me, because He hath anointed me to preach the gospel to the poor; He hath sent me to heal the brokenhearted, to preach deliverance to the captives, and recovering of sight to the blind, to set at liberty them that are bruised..." Third the death of Jesus Christ – Hebrews 9:14, "How much more shall the blood of Christ, who through the eternal Spirit offered himself without spot to God, purge your conscience from dead works to serve the living God?" And fourth the resurrection of Jesus – there are all 3 members of the Godhead that had a part in the resurrection. The Father, the Son and the Holy Ghost – Romans 1:4, "And declared to be the Son of God with power, according to the "spirit of holiness", by the resurrection from the dead..."

Chapter Twenty-One
Nine Gifts and Nine Fruits

◇◇◇◇◇

There are Nine Gifts of the Spirit Compared to the Nine Fruits of the Spirit - Too many people seek the Gifts without first acquiring the Fruit in their life. We must have the Fruit of the Spirit at work, if we want God to entrust us with the Gifts of the Spirit. Galatians 5:22-23 says, "But the fruit of the Spirit is love, joy, peace, patience (longsuffering), kindness, goodness, faithfulness, gentleness, and self-control." In 1 Cor. 12:8-10 speaks of the gifts, "To one there is given through the Spirit, the message of wisdom, to another the message of knowledge by means of the same Spirit, to another, Faith by the same Spirit, to another gifts of healing by the same Spirit, to another miraculous powers (working of miracles), to another prophecy, to another distinguishing between spirits (discerning of spirits), to another speaking in different kinds of tongues, and still another to interpretation of tongues."

The following is how the gifts of the Spirit and the fruits of the Spirit work together and how the fruits come first and the gifts are then given:

The fruits are: Love, Joy, Peace, Patience (longsuffering), Kindness, Goodness, Faithfulness, Gentleness, and Self-control.

The gifts are: Message of Wisdom, Message of Knowledge, Faith, Healing, Working of Miracles, Prophecy, Discerning of Spirits, Speaking in Tongues, and Interpretation of Tongues.

We can see how they work together.

1. If we have Wisdom of God (gift) we must first have Love the fruit of the Spirit. Searching for the gift of the Spirit first (Wisdom) will not come to us unless we possess the first fruit of the Spirit (Love). Love is the fruit and Wisdom is the gift.

2. Jesus gave instruction to His Disciples so His Joy would become a part of them. The fruit of the spirit is (Joy). The gift that comes with Joy is (A Word of Knowledge) which is received with Joy. Joy is the fruit and A Word of Knowledge is the gift.

3. If we have the (Peace) that passes all understanding then we have the fruit of the Spirit. We will be ready to receive (Faith) the gift of God. Supernatural faith is what releases miracles in our lives. Peace is the fruit and Faith if the gift.

4. God performs healings supernaturally. We learn from Patience (Long Suffering) to be content in any situation. Once we learn this fruit of the Spirit we are ready for the gift (Healing). Long Suffering is the fruit and Healing is the gift.

5. Working of Miracles comes from the Divine Power to do something that could not be done naturally. Jesus performed Miracles because he had the gift. When Jesus always acted with (Kindness) He already had the fruit of the Spirit. Without the fruit of (Kindness) we would not receive the gift. Kindness is the fruit and Performing Miracles is the gift. We use the gift how God would want us to.

6. When we are full of (Goodness) it means to have decency, generosity, and righteousness. We then have the fruit that claims the right to (Prophecy) the gift of the Spirit.

Prophecy (gift) is a sudden Spirit inspired insight. Goodness is the fruit of the Spirit and Prophecy is the gift of the Spirit.

7. The fruit of (Faithfulness) is the basis for being true only to our Lord. We then may seek the gift of (Discerning of Spirits) to further our knowledge of the working of the true Spirit of God. Faithfulness is the fruit and Discerning of spirits is the gift.

8. To be (Gentle) peaceful and pure is what the fruit of the Spirit offers us. We then can seek the gift (Different kinds of Languages) or you might say speaking in tongues. This is praying or singing in a supernatural or heavenly language. Gentleness is the fruit and Different kinds of Tongues are the gift.

9. God looks for people who have the fruit of (Self- Control) to be true and accurate. He will then give the gift of (Interpretation of tongues) to translate the Different Kinds of Tongues. Self-Control is the fruit and Interpretation of tongues is the gift of the Spirit. I like to call speaking in tongues "God's language."

Chapter Twenty-Two
The Baptism of the Holy Spirit

◇◇◇◇◇

To know more about the Holy Spirit we need to know more about how He works for us personally. We need the Baptism (or infilling) of the Holy Spirit. What it is, what it does for you, and how to receive it is a goal worth achieving. In the Old Testament prophecy concerning Baptism in the Holy Spirit is found in the book of Isaiah 28:11-12, "For it is with stammering lips and another tongue he will speak to this people, to whom he said, 'This is the rest with which you may cause the weary to rest', and 'This is refreshing', yet they would not hear." Also in the Old Testament in Joel 2:28-29 says, "And it shall come to pass afterward that I will pour out my Spirit on all flesh, your sons and your daughters shall prophesy, you old men shall dream dreams, you young men shall see visions. And also on my menservants and on my maidservants I will pour out my Spirit in those days."

In the New Testament we see the fulfillment of this prophecy in Acts 2:16-18 that refers to what the prophet Joel said about the baptism in the Holy Spirit. Also in the New Testament in John 1:32-34 tells us, "Then John gave this testimony: I saw the spirit come down from heaven as a dove and remain on him. I would not have known Him, except that the one who sent me to baptize with water told me.

'The man on whom you see the Spirit come down and remain is He who will baptize with the Holy Spirit.' I have seen and I testify that this is the Son of God."

We simply need to know more about the Holy Spirit. This actually has deepened my relationship with God, the Son and the Holy Spirit by just recognizing that I am related to the Godhead or the Holy Trinity. My load is much lighter as I walk my journey that leads me to the Cross by knowing that I am never alone and that I have the support of the three most important persons in my life – the Father, the Son, and the Holy Spirit.

This should be our goal in life to know what the gifts of the Spirit are and also what the fruits of the Spirit are. By knowing and using all the gifts and fruits we will have a closer walk with Jesus. Jesus emphasized the importance of being baptized in the Holy Spirit. This is the road to the Cross and on the way to the Cross we will always have the support of the Holy Spirit as our teacher and our guide.

The baptism of the Holy Spirit is for the purpose of empowering us for service, and is not for the purpose of cleansing us from our sins. We need to be careful NOT to value the gifts that we receive from God because the gifts will become idols. We must remember to value the one who has given the gifts to us.

Think again, what the fruits of the spirit are and what the gifts that are given after the fruits have become a part of our lives. We do not want to become so engrossed and focused on the gifts and fruits and forget where they come from. The fruits need to become a natural way of living just as breathing is a natural thing to sustain our lives. Never forget to thank Him for the fruits and the gifts.

I have made a list of what the fruits of the Spirit are and put them on my refrigerator to remind myself to constantly be aware of those attributes I need in my life to become a better person. I know that when the fruits become a natural part of me, God will see to it that the gifts will follow. I always give Him the glory, the honor, and the praise, and thank Him for His precious gifts.

Chapter Twenty-Three

Pray in the Spirit

◇◇◇◇◇

What does the baptism in the Holy Spirit do for you? First of all you speak to God. "For he who speaks in a tongue does not speak to man but to God, for no one understands him, however, in the spirit he speaks mysteries." (1 Cor. 14:2). When you allow the spirit to flow through you and you become edified or charged up spiritually, then speaking in tongues comes more like an automatic happening. "But you, beloved, building yourselves up on your most holy faith, praying in the Holy Spirit." (Jude 1:20)

There are times when we want to pray about a situation and yet we are not sure how to pray properly for a particular situation. It is certain that God will hear you if you chose to pray in the Spirit. In Romans 8:25, 27 it tells us, "Likewise the Spirit also helps in our weaknesses. For we do not know what we should pray for as we ought, but the Spirit Himself makes intercession for us with groanings which cannot be uttered. Now He who searches the hearts knows what the mind of the Spirit is, because He makes intercession for the saints according to the will of God."

When you repent and receive Christ as Savior, you are eligible to receive the baptism in the Holy Spirit. Peter denied Christ three times before receiving the baptism in the Holy Spirit, but on the day of Pentecost he had power and boldness to preach to the multitudes and 300 were born again. This really spoke straight into my heart and soul. I could think of times when I was not on the "straight and narrow" and had sin in my life, but when I did repent and receive Christ as my personal Savior, I was eligible to receive the baptism (the infilling) of the Holy Spirit. It all does not stop there. When I became aware of the baptism of the Holy Spirit (the infilling of the Holy Spirit) and allowed the Spirit to take over my being, I felt as though I was "drunk", and other times I began to shake when the power came down on me. I can always tell when the Spirit is in control because when I need to do something it becomes so much easier when you walk in the Spirit. You will find answers to many of your questions because the Spirit will always point the way, and be there to guide you.

Then there are times when you may be used in the gifts of the Spirit. The bible tells us in 1 Cor. 12:1-5, "Now about spiritual gifts, brothers, I do not want you to be ignorant. You know that when you were pagans, somehow or other you were influenced and led astray to mute idols. Therefore, I tell you that no one who is speaking by the Spirit of God says, "Jesus be cursed," and no one can say, "Jesus is Lord," except by the Holy Spirit. There are different kinds of gifts, but the same Spirit. There are different kinds of service, but the same Lord. There are different kinds of working, but the same God works all of them in all men." The gifts of the Holy Spirit are supernaturally given to individuals as the Spirit wills, so we cannot claim any permanent gifts of the Holy Spirit. We always want to use our gifts with love.

Remembering the fruits of the spirit - Love, Joy, Peace, Patience, Kindness, Goodness, Faithfulness, Gentleness, and Self-control, and how they must be a part of our lives before the gifts – Wisdom, Knowledge, Faith, Healing, Miraculous powers, Prophecy, Discerning of Spirits, Speaking in tongues, and Interpretation of tongues are received from God. He wants to know we can be trusted with the fruits and then the gifts will be granted to us.

Chapter Twenty-Four

Applying the Faith and Keeping the Faith

◇◇◇◇◇

Without FAITH we can be missing the baptism of the Holy Spirit. FAITH is all important to every individual in the Christian walk on the way to the Cross. FAITH keeps us close to God. FAITH keeps God close to us.

KEEP THE FAITH

Yes, FAITH when it is applied as proclaimed by the scriptures is when the Holy Spirit comes into our own lives. Hebrews 11:1-2 NIV Message Bible tells us, "The fundamental fact of existence is that this trust in God, this Faith, is the firm foundation under everything that makes life worth living. It is our handle on what we can't see."

"By faith Abel offered God a better sacrifice than Cain did. By faith he was commended as a righteous man, when God spoke well of his offerings. And by faith he still speaks, even though he is dead." (Heb. 11:4)

"And without faith it is impossible to please God, because anyone who comes to Him must believe that He exists and that he rewards those who earnestly seek Him." (Heb. 11:6)

"By faith Noah, when warned about things not yet seen, in holy fear built an ark to save his family. By his faith he condemned the world and became heir of the righteousness that comes by faith." (Heb. 11:7)

"By faith Abraham, even though he was past age – and Sarah herself was barren – was enabled to become a father because he considered him faithful who had made the promise. And so from this one man, and he as good as dead, came descendants as numerous as the stars in the sky and as countless as the sand on the seashore." (Heb. 11:11, 12)

"By faith Abraham, when God tested him, offered Isaac, as a sacrifice. He who had received promises was about to sacrifice his one and only son, even though God had said to him, "It is through Isaac that your offspring will be reckoned. Abraham reasoned that God could raise the dead, and figuratively speaking, he did receive Isaac back from death." (Heb. 11:17-19)

There are so many testimonies of what men of FAITH had endured, and accomplished that the Bible even says in Hebrews 11:32 through 35, "And what more shall I say? I do not have time to tell about Gideon, Barak, Samson, Jephthah, David, Samuel and the prophets, who through faith conquered kingdoms, administered justice, and gained what was promised; who shut the mouths of lions, quenched the fury of the flames, and escaped the edge of the sword; whose weakness and turned to strength; and who became powerful in battle and routed foreign armies. Women received back their dead, raised to life again. Others were tortured and refused to be released, so that they might gain a better resurrection."

There has been countless times in my life and I cannot list them all that it was by FAITH that I was able to be healed of a deadly disease. It was by FAITH I moved thousands of miles away from family. It was by FAITH I escaped death when being choked by an enraged husband. It was by FAITH I was able to design and build my own home. So many times I have been told by family and friends that I was foolish, but they were ones of little FAITH. It takes FAITH to continue on the way that leads us to the Cross.

Continue in FAITH even when the devil wants to control your life and wants to take away all your fruits and gifts you have received from the Spirit. With FAITH God will intervene to take back what the devil has stolen from you.

Chapter Twenty-Five
The Christian Walk

◇◇◇◇◇

On the way to the Cross, the Christian walk is not without problems and persecution by others who are not on the same walk with you. People will think things about you and their thoughts will not be very kind. They will say things to you and about you to others that are just plain cruel. One such thing that I have been called is, "She is nothing but a Jesus freak." That is when I thought of Jesus and how he had been scorned, humiliated, and ridiculed. I knew that Satan's goal is to take control of people's minds. I knew that Satan put those thoughts into people's minds. That is why I didn't care what others thought about me or what they may say about me. But I did care what God expects from me and what He thinks about me in my Christian walk with Him.

There are twists, turns, trials, and tribulations when we are being true to God. The devil is going to try all the harder to drive a wedge between us and God. The devil will use others to try to defeat us, to hurt us, to throw us off track in order to separate us from our relationship with the Father, the Son, and the Holy Spirit. In Matt 5:11-12 it explains it this way. "Blessed are you when people insult you, persecute you and falsely say all kinds of evil against you because of me. Rejoice and be glad because great is your reward in heaven, for in the same way they persecuted the prophets who were before you."

When we worry about what others are thinking or are saying about us, it takes our energy and our thoughts away from the better things in life and what the Cross represents. It takes us away from what God wants for us.

Chapter Twenty-Six

The Evil One

◇◇◇◇◇

It is important for us to know and understand the workings of Satan...the evil one...the prince of darkness and what he can do to wreak havoc in our lives. We need to know how to eliminate Satan from our lives. Satan knows how to use the flesh to get what he wants. He will get in the minds of God's children to manipulate and control the behavior of all of us mortals.

Who is Satan? Where did he come from? How does he know so much? "How art thou fallen from heaven, O Lucifer, son of the morning! How art thou cut down to the ground, which didst weaken the nations! For thou hast said in thine heart, I will ascend into heaven, I will exalt my throne above the stars of God: I will sit also upon the mount of the congregation, in the sides of the north: I will ascend above the heights of the clouds; I will be like the most High." (Isaiah 14:12-14KJV)

The bible says that Satan (Lucifer) was God's most powerful of His angels. Sometime after Lucifer's creation and before mankind was created, Lucifer (Satan) rebelled against God. Satan took one third of the angels with him. These angels are now referred to as demons.

Before his fall, Satan was created as a perfect being and was wise and completely righteous. It was Satan's pride that caused him to fall. He wanted to receive the worship due to God alone. Satan and one third of the angels rebelled against God. The archangel, Michael, fought with God's angels against Satan. Satan lost the battle, and he was cast from heaven down to earth.

When Satan went into the Garden of Eden, he became a snake where he tempted Eve to eat from the Tree of Knowledge of good and evil. She believed Satan's lie that she would become like God. Adam was nowhere around to be able to protect Eve from making that mistake of disobeying God's instruction not to eat from the Tree of Knowledge. Later, Adam followed his wife's lead and he, too, ate from the Tree of Knowledge which was their downfall. God evicted them from the Garden of Eden.

Satan is nothing but a snake and he can convince us to make the same mistake of disobeying God's instruction the same as Adam and Eve did in the Garden of Eden. They paid for their disobeying God' instruction, and the consequences they received was to be cast out of the Garden of Eden. We will, too, if we choose to believe Satan's lies.

Chapter Twenty-Seven

Jesus vs. Satan

◇◇◇◇◇

When I think of Jesus and compare Him to Satan it is very obvious that Satan opposes Jesus Christ – who is God that took on the form of a man to redeem humanity from their sin. So I look at what Jesus would do and that is to lead people to salvation. Then I look at Satan and see that he leads people into rebellion. Jesus's method would be to tell people the truth. And then seeing Satan, he would tell a person lies. Jesus would teach love whereas Satan would teach hate. When people would follow Jesus they would know love, joy, peace, patience, kindness, goodness, faithfulness, gentleness and self-control. When people would fall into Satan's trap they would know sexual immorality, impurity, debauchery, idolatry, witchcraft, hatred, discord, jealousy, selfish ambition, envy, drunkenness, and orgies. So what would be the end result from following Jesus? It would be freedom from sin. Then what would be the result from following Satan? It would be enslavement to sin.

This is what Jesus has to say about Satan's power, "I saw Satan fall like lightning from heaven. I have given you authority to trample on snakes and scorpions and to overcome all the power of the enemy; nothing will harm you. However, do not rejoice that the *spirits submit to you, but rejoice that your names are written in heaven."* (Luke 10: 18-20)

I know that Satan hates the Word of God and the name of Jesus because Jesus destroys everything that Satan stands for. Because Jesus gave us the authority we need to use it by saying the words in a firm expression and also believing that, Satan you are defeated in the name of Jesus! I rebuke you in the name of Jesus! I am a child of the Most High God and Satan you have no authority over my life and you are under my feet. You are the tail and not the head. I believe and have faith that Satan is eliminated when we speak out against him in the name of Jesus.

Using the Bible we get specific instructions about resisting the devil/Satan"

> "Submit therefore to God. Resist the devil and he will flee from you." (James 4:7)

> "In your anger do not sin: Do not let the sun go down while you are still angry, and do not give the devil a foothold." (Eph. 4:26-27)

> "In addition to all this, take up the shield of faith, with which you can extinguish all the flaming arrows of the evil one." (Eph. 6:16)

> "Be of sober spirit, be on the alert. Your adversary, the devil, prowls around like a roaring lion, seeking someone to devour. But resist him, firm in your faith, know that the same experiences of suffering are being accomplished by your brethren who are in the world." (1Peter 5:8-9)

In Matthew 1:1-11 we find that Satan tried to win Jesus over and wanted Jesus to worship him. "Then Jesus was led up by the Spirit into the wilderness to be tempted by the devil. And after He had fasted forty days and forty nights, He then became hungry. And the tempter came and said to Him, 'If You are the Son of God, command that theses stones become bread.' But He answered and said, 'It is written, 'MAN SHALL NOT LIVE ON BREAD ALONE, BUT ON EVERY WORD THAT PROCEEDS OUT OF THE MOUTH OF GOD.' Then the devil took Him into the holy city and had Him stand on the pinnacle of the temple, and said to Him, "If You are the Son of God, throw Yourself down; for it is written, 'HE WILL COMMAND HIS ANGELS CONCERNING YOU'; and "ON their HANDS THEY WILL BEAR YOU UP, SO THAT YOU WILL NOT STRIKE YOUR FOOT AGAINST A STONE.' Jesus said to him, 'On the other hand, it is written, "YOU SHALL NOT PUT THE LORD YOUR GOD TO THE TEST.' Again, the devil took Him to a very high mountain and showed Him all the kingdoms of the world and their glory; and he said to Him, 'All these things I will give you, if You fall down and worship me.' Then Jesus said to him, "Go, Satan! For it is written, 'YOU SHALL WORSHIP THE LORD YOUR GOD, AND SERVE HIM ONLY.' Then the devil left Him; and behold, angels came and began to minister to Him."

This scripture shows me and tells me how Satan will not give up and will try time and time again in his effort to tempt us, to deceive us, to try to have us worship him. Jesus shows us the way and He quotes the Word of God and then demands Satan to go! This is the perfect example we need to follow whenever Satan tries to ensnare us.

Chapter Twenty-Eight
Enemies of the Cross

◇◇◇◇◇

The Christian walk is the way of the Cross. There are times when we can fall short of our goals and aspirations. It is a fact that as humans we will fall short of the Christian walk because while we are still in the flesh, we do yield to temptation and discipline fails to keep us on the right plane with God. In 1 Cor. 1: 18 it says, "For the message of the Cross is foolishness to those who are perishing, but to us who are being saved it is the power of God." God knew we needed a Savior. God knew He had to come to earth in the flesh as Jesus to show us the way. God knew He had to have Jesus save us from Satan's trap. Satan cannot condemn us when we have the faith in Jesus. Jesus paid the full price for our sins – He paid it all! Jesus died because of our sins and God deserted the sinful human part of Jesus when he was on the Cross. Jesus descended into hell before He ascended to be with his Father in heaven. Jesus left all the sins in the devil's hell. We have been saved from hell by what Jesus did on the Cross.

Satan will do anything to divert us from our spiritual path we are on that leads us to the Cross. Satan knows how to use the flesh to get what he wants. He knows how to set traps for us to fall into his carnal ways. He can make things seem so promising and when he knows he has you, he will pull the rug out from under you and leave you in a life of misery. Every person on this planet is subject to the evil ploys of Satan. He works in the minds of his prey both male and female. He will take control of a person's mind and then he gains control of the physical being.

There are enemies of the Cross that we need to be aware of in our Christian walk. There are people who can "talk the talk", but they have a hard time to "walk the walk." We must be on guard when we start focusing on our own selves. We must be on guard when we promote our own worthiness - that is an enemy of the Cross. We need to be on guard when we boast of our accomplishments – that is an enemy of the Cross. We need to be on guard when we promote our own righteousness – that is an enemy of the Cross. We need to be on guard when we are tempted by saying words and doing deeds that are against what Jesus taught – those are enemies of the Cross. The Cross will become of no effect when we reduce ourselves to a level that goes against the glory of God. The Cross becomes a big fat zero when we choose the way of the world. The way of the Cross is following the teachings of Jesus and why He died for us on the Cross.

Chapter Twenty-Nine

The choices you make will lead you to which one?

◇◇◇◇◇

When we look at pictures of the cross such as a picture of the three crosses on a hill, there is a story that each cross can tell. What will our stories be like and what Cross will we end up at? Jesus died on the Cross that was in the middle of two criminals. Jesus followed the will of His Father and focused His life so that His life style would glorify God. The two criminals followed the ways of the world and chose the ways of Satan which was a dark and dismal life style.

One of the criminals was talking to the Roman guards, "What did he do, murder someone?" When the thief asked the soldier, I would imagine that the answer from that question was to say that Jesus committed a worse crime than the criminals. The guard said, "This man, Jesus, did not murder or rob people, He calls Himself the Son of God."

I think that the soldier must have thought that Jesus was a fool to claim such a thing. Then the soldier must have had the mind set as to what his job was to do and that was to see to it that the three will die no matter if they were a king, a Jew, or a Gentile. Then the soldier began to carry out his duty to nail all three to their Crosses.

Chapter Thirty
Line Up Your "T's"

◇◇◇◇◇

L ooking at the Crosses we can see three giant T's. These T's can represent a number of words that start with the letter "T", and we can learn which of those "T words" we can use in our Christian walk. It all amounts to the choices we will make on a daily basis. Will we make choices that will line up our "T's"

that will lead us to the Cross of Jesus? Or will we make choices that will line up our "T's" so that we will end up on one of the two other crosses?

As an example, I chose the following words that begin with the letter "T": Truth, Trust, Transition, Time, Transcend, Transformation, Teach, Temporary, Temptation, Temple, Travel, and Thanksgiving. There are others, but these are the words that start with "T" that means the most to me. This is how I would line up my "T's" on my way to the Cross. These words all have a significant meaning to me. There are other interpretations for these words; however, I chose to give them meaning for specific reasons.

TRUTH

As a child I learned about truth from my father. He taught me to always tell the truth. His words of wisdom about truth had meaning to me. He told me to tell the truth because you will never have to remember what you said. He said that when you tell a lie you will have to tell ten lies to cover up the first lie. You will have to remember each lie that you told in order to make the first lie seem like the truth, and then another lie to cover that one, and then remember that lie when you tell the next lie and on and on. It is so much better to tell the truth in the first place, and then you do not have to remember what you said. I wanted to know what Jesus would say about the truth. There are many scriptures in the Bible that are spoken in regards to truth. Jesus learned His truth from His Father. Jesus was talking to the Jews when He said, "If you hold to my teaching, you are really my disciples. Then you will know the truth and the truth will set you free" (John 8:31-32).

TRUST

When I trust someone, I have faith in them, I have confidence in them, but in the human world they can let me down. It was when I found Jesus I knew that my trust and faith were well founded. "Trust in the Lord with all your heart and lean not on your own understanding; in all your ways acknowledge him, and he will make your paths straight" (Proverbs 3:5).

TRANSITION

Making a transition is a time of change. Change was something that I, at one time, feared. As I observed and became more aware of what was going on around me I could easily see on the outside of my being, but more importantly I needed to be aware of the subtleties happening on the inside of my being. I found that transition, change, and awareness are essential for my spiritual growth. I had to surrender to God for Him to work His wonders in me. I no longer feared change. God's creation reflects changes. The seasons show changes from summer to fall, and from fall to winter and from winter to spring, and from spring to summer.

TIME

When we look at God's time, it has nothing to do with our clocks, our calendars, our weeks or our months. God has all of eternity at His disposal. Scripture tells us, "There is a time for everything, and a season for every activity under heaven: a time to be born and a time to die, a time to plant and a time to uproot, a time to kill and a time to heal, a time to tear down and a time to build, a time to weep and a time to laugh, a time to mourn and a time to dance, a time to scatter stones and a time to gather them, a time to embrace and a time to refrain, a time to keep and a time to throw away, a time to tear and a time to mend, a time to be silent and a time to speak, a time to love and a time to hate, a time for war and a time for peace" (Eccl 3:1-8).

TRANSCEND

To be able to rise above a given situation the same as Jesus did when he was faced with his torture and crucifixion. This word has a specific meaning to me. As a child I was abused by an older brother. He would say things and do things that were harmful to me emotionally and physically. I used to cry a lot and that even led to more teasing and ridicule. I used to have nightmares that someone was trying to get me and was chasing me. I was outside in the dream and I was running as fast as my legs would carry me. I ran into someone's back yard and all of a sudden I ran into a very high wooden fence. I panicked because I knew the person pursuing me would have me trapped in the yard. I turned around to see who it was that was chasing me, and I saw that it was my brother. As soon as I saw who it was, I felt myself rising up above the tall fence, and in my child's mind I thought it must be a person lifting me. It was not so, but that dream came to serve me in other situations when I knew I had to exist above and independent of the situation that was harmful. Another incident that helped me to see the lesson of that dream/nightmare came to me in another dream/nightmare. There was a bully in the neighborhood that would torment me whenever I was outside with my skates on. He would threaten me that he was going to knock me off my feet. I tried to stay away from him, but he kept following me wherever I went. The dream/nightmare I had involved a train that was coming towards me and I ran as hard and fast as I could, but I had no way to get away from the train. I experienced the same sensation of floating and rising above the dangerous situation. I believe that the Holy Spirit was showing me through my dreams that it is a way of dealing with life's problems and situations that I have no control over. Transcend or rise above it and let it pass because it will surely go away in time.

TRANSFORMATION

The first thing that I think of is the butterfly. In the beginning it was a caterpillar that crawls on the ground and it feeds and it grows, and then it spins a cocoon around itself. When it's time is right it emerges from the cocoon in a very different form. It now has wings and is no longer bound to the earth. In scripture it tells us, "And be not conformed to this world, but be ye transformed by the renewing of your mind, that ye may prove what is that good, and acceptable, and perfect, will of God" (Romans 12:2).

TEACH

Teach only love because that is what we are. That is how God created us with His love. Jesus taught us by the example he set for us to follow. Jesus taught us from the very beginning of His life to the very end when He made His way to the Cross. The Holy Spirit is always present to teach us. We need to be open to receive from Him because we are not always aware that He is available to us.

Everyone is a teacher. We are always learning from others or we are teaching others. We teach through our behavior. We teach through the words we speak. We teach through our actions. If we are not teaching, we are learning. Yes, we also learn from ourselves so we are our own teachers. Jesus and the Holy Spirit are the greatest teachers of all. They teach us God's truth. Speaking to Moses, God said, "Who gave man his mouth? Who makes him deaf or mute? Who gives him sight or makes him blind? Is it not I, the Lord? Now go; I will help you speak and will *TEACH* you what to say." (Exodus 4:11-12)

TEMPORARY

This too will pass. Our life on this planet is only temporary. Nothing on this earth is permanent. Everything on this earth will some day pass away. The only thing real is God's love. It is forever.

God is in control of all eternity, and we can have eternal life when we believe in HIM. "For God so loved the world that He gave His one and only Son, that whoever believes in Him shall not perish, but have eternal life." (John 3:16)

TEMPTATION

In the Lord's prayer it tells us: Lead us not into temptation, but deliver us from evil…" This is Satan's way to try and keep us from God. We must be on guard in order to bypass temptation. Only Jesus can save us. Keep the Faith.

TEMPLE

My temple is my body temple. This is where my spirit resides while living on this planet. I am required to care for my temple and to keep it healthy in order to be a good servant for the Lord. When I no longer need my earthly temple, then I will be homeward bound to my heavenly temple to live with Jesus.

TRAVEL

As we travel through our life it is inevitable that we be obedient to the Lord. We must follow where He leads us both physically and spiritually. Jesus traveled about doing good and spreading the Word of God.

THANKSGIVING

We humble ourselves and thank the Lord for all that He has done for us. We give Him all the praise, the honor, and the glory. He has bestowed a multitude of blessings upon us. We are forever in His debt. We thank Him for His Son, Jesus, and how He died for us because of our sins.

Chapter Thirty-One

We Are Not Our Bodies

◇◇◇◇◇

W e continue to learn from Jesus from the time when He walked the earth, when He hung on the Cross, and when He is in the spirit world at the right side of God. We are spirit the same as Christ is. We are not our bodies, we are spirit. At the time we were born God breathed His spirit into us giving us life. "The Lord God formed the man from the dust of the ground and breathed into his nostrils the breath of life, and the man became a living being" (Genesis 2:7). We need to focus on the Holy Spirit and the fruits of the Spirit and how to use the gifts of the Spirit. They are always there and at our disposal when we walk the path that leads us to the Cross. Never forget to give thanks for the multitude of blessings that the Godhead has bestowed upon us. Through the spirit we can receive and know what God's plan is for us.

We live in a natural world and most people tend to divorce the natural life from the spiritual life. We are a natural human being and we live in a natural world. We are a spiritual being also. We need to learn how to combine the two and allow God to become the force in our lives.

When I am in the need of healing, I realize that I am not my body. It is my flesh that is sick and I do not focus on what is wrong in my body because I am spirit. Jesus Christ is spirit, God is spirit, the Holy Spirit is spirit and we are spirit. I focus on my spirit because this is where my healing will take place. Healing then can manifest in the body. Then I affirm that I am healed in the name of Jesus, and believe with all my being that it is so. By His stripes we are healed. He sees us as whole and healthy. We need to affirm that we are whole and healthy and get it into our spirit and believe it is so.

Chapter Thirty-Two

Practice the Present

◇◇◇◇◇

The Father, Son and the Holy Spirit are always present in the present moment. When we practice the present we will always be in the presence of the Godhead.

We will be in connection with the Holy Trinity. Living in the moment means we are not thinking about the future. Living in the moment means we are not thinking about the past. This is what I call "Living in the Eternal Now." We are living in the presence with the Father, the Son, and the Holy Spirit when we are "practicing the present".

Now is when we are living. Now is when we need something to carry us through turbulent times. Be still and Know that I am God is what the bible tells us. When we connect with God in "His time" it is going to be easier for us to rise above the situation and find the answers needed to pull us through. When we connect with God in "His time" He can lift us up to a higher level when the worldly efforts are dragging us down. At this higher vantage point with God we can get a wider view of the world. Not in a one dimensional view. Not in a two dimensional view. Not in a three dimensional view, but in a "multidimensional" view that will show us the way, the truth and the life.

Staying in the now or practicing the present gives us the opportunity to hear the voice of God. How precious is this time that we spend with our Lord. This is an intimate moment just being one on one with our most high God. This is when He becomes the only God before us. There is no other God and the whole world is put on "hold" when we are in this present moment. This is putting God first. This is connecting with Him in our secret place.

This develops a very deep and personal relationship with the Godhead. This relationship needs to have continued renewal every day. This will guarantee us the strength we will need in times of crisis and tribulation. This is like having a personal revival to lift us to the heights where Satan or the world will have no influence on us, on our spirits, on our emotions, on our minds, and also it gives the body a chance to relax.

My personal experience with practicing the present was when I learned to meditate. At that particular time in my life, meditation was foreign to me and I had no concept as to how to go about doing it. I was working for a large Government agency and the job I had was very stressful. I went to the doctor to find out if there was anything I could do to relieve the stress in my life. At first the doctor wanted to give me some drugs for my problem. I refused to take any medication and then I told the doctor that he could not help me. To my surprise the doctor changed his whole demeanor and had me sit and he began to talk to me about meditation. He did not give me any instructions as to how to begin so I went to the book store and purchased several books on meditation. It was apparent that some of the techniques were not suitable for me. I finally found one that suited my life style and then began the process of meditation. My first attempt was to focus on Jesus, and I would spend an hour each day to meditate. After several days it became a thirst and I couldn't wait to get home from work to start my meditation. I soon learned that I didn't need to be at home to meditate, but I would grab a few minutes whenever I could to listen and practice the present. Meditation to me is listening to God. Prayer to me is talking to God.

Chapter Thirty-Three

The Voice of God

◇◇◇◇◇

This was the beginning of my realization that I could hear the Voice of God. In the stillness away from the world I could allow the messages to come clearer. Jesus could hear the voice of God, and He knew the difference between God's voice and what was not the Voice of God. Jesus was obedient to God and listened to His voice. Jesus became Gods Word in action. Obedience, faith, and love for His Father were sufficient for Jesus on His way to the Cross.

There are times that God will speak audibly, then there are times His voice comes as a spontaneous thought, or a vision, or it could be a feeling, and sometimes it is just an impression. Our job is to discern and recognize that it is truly the Voice of God. As we spend time with Jesus we will gradually come to recognize His Voice. Satan always wants to put in his two cents. We must be alert to know the difference between what the Lord says and what the devil is saying. Once you know the Lord's voice so very well, you will not be fooled by other voices.

Cindy Jacobs wrote the book "The Voice of God", and she said, "This book will not give you a specific formula describing the prophetic call and the way to hear the Voice of God. God's methods *are unique. However, I hope to give you some signposts to follow. One thing I have learned through the years is that not all prophetic calls are alike. Each person is unique in his or her gifts and abilities. The ways of God, kneaded into our lives through Holy Spirit-appointed visitations and circumstances, have molded each of us in a different fashion. (The Voice of God by Cindy Jacobs, copyright date 1995 by Cindy Jacobs. Published by Chosen Books a division of Baker Publishing Group, Grand Rapids, Michigan.*

Anyone interested in learning more about the voice of God would benefit by reading Cindy Jacobs book, "The Voice of God".

Those who will spend a profound awareness that God does speak to us, they will be in a wonderful position to receive His Word. Satan will always want us to use our own power and not the "Power of God", and when we receive a direction through His Voice we need to know it is His guidance. When we get direction from the Lord there are times that we will have to step outside our comfort zone with Faith that all things are possible when we focus on God's will, and what His Voice directs us to do. What God will want from me can be very different from what He will ask of someone else. This is because people are widely varied and molded and God knows whom to call for an appointed service.

It is so important to remember in our Christian walk on the way to the Cross that Satan would like to plant ideas in our heads that God has favorites and he would try to convince us that we could not be able to hear the Voice of God. Satan does not want us to hear God – Satan wants us to disobey and rebel against Him.

A word to the wise about false prophets who claim they hear the Voice of God. In Matt. 7:15-18, 20 it tell us, "Beware of false prophets who come to you in sheep's clothing, but inwardly they are ravenous wolves. You will know them by their fruits. Do men gather grapes from thorn bushes or figs from thistles? Even so, every good tree bears good fruit, but a bad tree bears bad fruit. A good tree cannot bear bad fruit, nor can a bad tree bear good fruit...Therefore by their fruits you will know them."

God will speak to us in supernatural ways. He desires to

be involved intimately in our lives and He wants to answer our questions. He wants to protect us and give us the guidance we would want from Him. We must realize that when we become still we will know it is God. "Be still, and know that I am God." (Psalm 46:10) Become still so you can sense God's flow of thoughts and emotions within our being. If we are not still, we will sense only our own thoughts, and the thoughts that come from worldly sources. Learn to listen to the voice of God who dwells in the center (heart) of your being. To see visions, you must see with the eyes in your heart (center) of your being because God gave you your "inner ears" to hear and your "inner eyes" to see and thus to know the Voice of God.

When I think about hearing the voice of God, it feels to me like a responsibility, a gift, or a loving message from our most high God. Lord have mercy on me when I do not listen to that small voice within my being and instead, follow my own understanding. It is too late when I realize I didn't "listen" or heed His voice. When I realize this, I have to work at climbing out of the hole I made for myself.

I have no one to blame for my mistake. I must learn from my mistakes and take up my Cross and continue in faith.

.

Chapter Thirty-Four

Pray

◇◇◇◇◇

Throughout my writings I have touched on the Crucifixion of Christ, the resurrection of Christ, the Cross, the Holy Spirit, faith, believing, practicing the presence, love, forgiveness, surrendering, trust, truth, temptation, transformation, transition, and teaching, etc. all of which can be related to Jesus and His life on earth. In many ways our lives parallel from us to the life of Jesus the Christ while He lived on earth in a human body. When Jesus is our focus, we will always be on the path that leads us to the Cross.

The one area of Christ's life that I want to express the importance of and that is prayer. The Scriptures talk about prayer and praying in the Old Testament and in the New Testament. My favorite scripture comes from Matthew. "And when you pray, do not be like the hypocrites, for they love to pray standing in the synagogues and on the street corners to be seen by men. I tell you the truth, they have received their reward in full. But when you pray, go into your room, close the door and pray to your Father, who is unseen. Then your Father, who sees what is done in secret, will reward you. And when you pray, do not keep on babbling like pagans, for they think they will be heard because of their many words. Do not be like them, for your Father knows what you need before you ask him. This, then, is how you should pray:

Our Father in heaven,
Hallowed be your name,
Your kingdom come,
Your will be done
On earth as it is in heaven.
Give us today our daily bread.
Forgive us our debts,
As we also have forgiven our debtors.
And lead us not into temptation,
But deliver us from the evil one."
(Matt. 6:5-13)

The disciples knew something of Christ's wonderful life in public. They knew of His connection with His secret life of prayer. The disciples saw Him as a Master in the art of prayer. No one could pray like Jesus did. The disciples would ask Him to teach them to pray. "Lord, teach us to pray." (Luke 11:1)

We may wonder at times if there is something unacceptable about praying for everyday personal and family matters or concerns – health, money, and protection. Absolutely not, because Jesus taught us to pray, "Give us this day our daily bread." When we follow Jesus's example we can acknowledge our need for God's down-to-earth favors and help.

Not all of us will pray in exactly the same way. God yearns for all of us to pray to Him. Be still and know that He is God. These quiet moments can help you shift gears from other interests to God and His interests. Avoid rushing through the prayer. You may want to pause often to hold your requests before the Lord.

Chapter Thirty-Five
Types of Prayer

◇◇◇◇◇

There are different types of prayers. We at times pray a personal prayer such as a prayer of commitment to ask for forgiveness or to forgive someone, to be more loving, or to live free from worry. Another type of personal prayer is a prayer for personal concerns such as for a spouse or children, home, prosperity, or health.

Another type of prayer is the intercessory prayers for others. They can be prayers for God's people and ministers. They can be prayers for the World. They can be prayers for the needs of others. When the prayers are within God's Will, they will be answered.

There are things we need to be aware of when we pray. Be specific and stand on God's promises. You must ask God for what you want. Be positive in your thinking and reject anything that contradicts the Word. See yourself with your answers, and continually thank God for the answers. Make your prayer a statement of faith.

It is important to keep joy in our hearts at all times. By that, I mean we keep joy BEFORE our prayers to our heavenly Father. We need to continue to have joy even if we are waiting for an answer to our prayers. When we know when our prayers are answered and even if they are not answered, we need to continually keep a joyful attitude. It may be easier to have joy when prayers are answered vs. when they are not answered. It is very important that we express our gratitude and thanksgiving to our generous Lord. From our grateful hearts we need to thank Him in advance for what we are to receive. In the bible Jesus says, "So with you. Now is your time of grief, but I will see you again and you will rejoice, and no one will take away your joy. In that day you will no longer ask me anything, I tell you the truth, my Father will give you whatever you ask in my name. Ask and you will receive, and your joy will be complete." (John 16:22-24)

Chapter Thirty-Six
In the Name of Jesus

◇◇◇◇◇

When we conclude our prayers we want to tell our Father that we pray in the name of Jesus. Jesus gave us the right and the authority to use His name in prayer. Jesus' name has the authority and is the key. Use the key and the key does the work. He gave us the authority when we pray, when we cast out the devil, when we call out demons that bind men's souls with darkness and disease.

Once we pray we must not worry because worry can only block God's answers to our prayers. Just remember that God does not command us, "Pray!" and then stand back to see if we will obey. He invites us - - He welcomes us - - into the high privilege of talking and working with Him. He provides us with the enabling power of the Holy Spirit within us and gives us guidance for fruitful prayer in the Bible. He even encourages us through other Christians who are on the same walk with us as we continue On the Way to the Cross.

Chapter Thirty-Seven

In Conclusion

◇◇◇◇◇

I n conclusion, I would like to say that the Power of the Cross's greatest lesson for me that Jesus taught me was when He was on the cross. The lesson is to surrender, to give in to, relinquish, and release my spirit to God. I Give it all to God and see what He can do in my life. I trust what God can do in my life. I surrender control to Him. This is what I learned as I continue On The Way to the Cross. I remember that when I surrender or release everything to God, it doesn't let me off the hook to not do my part. I am in partnership with God and it requires me to work with him and not to sit back and expect Him to do all the work.

I can relate to the Apostle Paul when he wrote to the Philippians when he tells them to "stand fast", to be of the same mind, to rejoice in the Lord always, to make known your requests through prayer and to know the peace of God and to renew your hearts and minds through Christ Jesus.

"Not that I have already obtain all this, or have already been made perfect, but I press on to take hold of that for which Christ Jesus took hold of me. Brothers, I do not consider myself yet to have taken hold of it. But one thing I do: Forgetting what is behind and

straining toward what is ahead. I press on toward the goal to win the prize for which God has called me heavenward in Christ Jesus.

All of us who are mature should take such view of things. And if on some point you think differently, that too God will make clear to you. Only let us live up to what we have already attained.

Join with others in following my example, brothers, and take note of those who live according to the pattern we gave you. For, as I have often told you before and now say again even with tears, many live as enemies of the cross of Christ. Their destiny is destruction, their god is their stomach, and their glory is in their shame. Their mind is on earthly things. But our citizenship is in heaven. And we eagerly await a Savior from there, the Lord Jesus Christ, who by the power that enables Him to bring everything under His control will transform our lowly bodies so that they will be like his glorious body" (Phil 3:12-21).

Just as Paul said to the Philippians, I, too, will continue to press on toward my goal as a citizen of heaven and wait for my Savior to lead me home. And while I am waiting I will continue my endeavor to be more like Jesus the Christ in whatever I do or whatever I say during my journey On the Way to the Cross.

Bibliography

Acts 2:16-18 Holy Bible

1 Corinthians 1:18, the Holy Bible; New International Version (NIV)

1 Corinthians 5:7 NIV

1Corinthians 12:1-5; NIV

1Corinthians12:8-10; NIV

1 Corinthians 13:1-13, the Holy Bible; King James Version (KJV)

1Corinthians 14:2; NIV

2Corinthians 5:21; NIV

Ecclesiastes 3:1-8; NIV

Ephesians 4:26, 27; NIV

Exodus 4:11, 12; NIV

Ezekiel 37:27; NIV

Galatians 5:16, 22-23; NIV

Genesis 1:2; NIV

Genesis 2:7; NIV

Genesis 22:2, the Holy Bible; New Living Translation, second edition; (NLT)

Hebrews 9:14; NIV

Hebrews 11:1-2: NIV

Hebrews 11:4; NIV

Hebrews 11:7; NIV

Hebrews 11:11, 12; NIV

Hebrews 11:17-19; NIV

Hebrews 11:32—35; NIV

Isaiah 14:12-14; NIV

James 4:7; NIV

Joel 2:28, 29; NIV

John 1:32-34; NIV

John 3:16; NIV

John 3:16-18, the Holy Bible; NIV Message Bible

John 8:31-32; NIV

John 14:2; NIV

John 14:25-26; NIV

John 15:7; NIV

John 16:13; KJV

John 16:19-22; NIV

John 16:22-24; NIV

John 16:19-22; NIV

John 19:26-27; NIV

John 19:28; NIV

John 19:29-30; NIV

John 20:19-20; NIV

1John 4:4-6; KJV

Jude 1:20; NIV

Luke 4:1; NIV

Luke 4:18; NIV

Luke 10:18-20; NIV

Luke 11:1; NIV

Luke22:39-44; NIV

Luke 22:63-65; NIV

Luke 23:24; NIV

Luke 23:32-33; NIV

Luke 23:42; NIV

Luke 23:39-43; NIV

Luke 23:44; NIV

Mark 1:7-8; NIV

Mark 12:29-31; NIV

Mark 15:12-14; NIV

Mark 15:14; NIV

Mark 15:19-20; NIV

Mark 15:34; NIV

Matthew 1:20; NIV

Matthew 1:1-11 NIV

Matthew 2:5; NIV

Matthew 5:11, 12; NIV

Matthew 6:5-13; NIV

Matthew 6:12; NIV

Matthew 7:7-8; NIV

Matthew 7:15-18; NIV

Matthew 26:17; NIV

Matthew 26:64; NIV

Matthew 27:46; NIV

Matthew 27:51; NIV

Matthew 27:54; NIV

Matthew 28:1-7; NIV

Matthew 28:18-20; NIV

Merriam-Webster Dictionary – First pocket books printing – August 1974

PATH TO THE CRUCIFIXION – Crucifixion of Jesus, Wikepedia, the free encyclopedia; copied from the internet: http://en.wikepedia.org

1 Peter 2:24; NIV

1Peter 5:7; NIV

1Peter 5:8, 9; NIV

2 Peter 1:20-21; NIV

Philippians 3:12-21; NIV

Philippians 4:4-7; NIV

Proverbs 3:5; NIV

Proverbs 22:6; KJV

Psalms 46:10; NIV

RELATIONSHIP PRINCIPLES OF JESUS – copyrighted in 2008 by author, Tim Holladay; Zondervan, Grand Rapids, Michigan www.zondervan.com

Romans 1:4; NIV

Romans 8:25-27; NIV

Romans 12:2; NIV

1Timothy 2:5-6; NIV

THE PURPOSE DRIVEN LIFE – copyrighted in 2002 by author Rick Warren; Zondervan, Grand Rapids, Michigan www.zondervan.com

THE VOICE OF GOD, copyrighted 1995 by Cindy Jacobs, published by Chosen Books a division of Baker Publishing Group, Grand Rapids, Michigan

Vines Concise Dictionary of the Bible – copyright 1997, 1999 by Thomas Nelson, Inc.

OTHER BOOKS WRITTEN BY DR. PATRICIA LOUISE WILSON

AUTHOR NAME: PATRICIA LOUISE
PONDERING
THE REFLECTIONS
OF LIFE
AND
THE REFLECTIONS OF LOVE

Published by Westbow Press
A Division of
Thomas Nelson & Zondervan

About the Author

I received my bachelor's degree in ministry, my master's in Christian education, and my doctorate in theology. I worked in the ministry and spent time in the education field, but my passion is writing. My creator, my healer, my savior, and my messenger—the Holy Spirit—has prompted me to continue writing. You will enjoy how my writing reflects all of them.

9 781512 724134